Here Be Dragons

By the same author

Poetry

One Tree Bridge
(chapbook, TLYT Publications, PA, US)

As Co-editor

Voices from the Parking Lot
(The Parkinson Alliance, Princeton, NJ, US)

Here Be Dragons

Dennis Greene

PUNCHER & WATTMANN

First published in 2015

Published by Puncher and Wattmann
PO Box 441
Glebe NSW 2037

http://www.puncherandwattmann.com
puncherandwattmann@bigpond.com

National Library of Australia
Cataloguing-in-Publication entry:

Greene, Dennis

Here Be Dragons

ISBN   9781922186706

I. Title.

A821.3

Cover design by Matthew Holt

Printed by McPherson's Printing Group

This project has been assisted by the Western Australian Government through the Department of Culture and the Arts

Government of **Western Australia**
Department of **Culture and the Arts**

To Jo

Contents

'What then?' sang Plato's ghost, 'what then?'

W.B. Yeats

One Tree Bridge

That first morning, hoping to catch the dawn,
we stepped instead into a world of mist
and dark green forest, mixed with the softer
greys of smoke from pot-bellied stoves, and
the light green of the ferns along the river.

Taken by mist the road could not be seen,
though what remained of the one-log bridge
that gave this place its name moved through
degrees of sight right on the edge of seen,
unseen, just seen: a bridge into infinity, a lost
road, vanished, dreamed, now going nowhere.

And we, my child and I, being small and quiet,
watched as from drifts of mist the great trees
grew, regained their shapes, their varied colours,
their forty-metre stretch that touched the sky,
and took it in, each from our own perspective:
she from the bridge, I from a long-gone road.

Preparing the Way

I will take the locusts
and the wild honey
to the vacant lot
behind the health food store
and eat them there,
alone while waiting
under the shade of trees
graffitied on the wall.

I've been thinking lately
that the things I'm saying
when I speak my mind
to people passing through
should be more in line
with new millennium thinking
unless you think
the same old lines will do.

Oh by the way
for quite some time now
I've been waiting
and the headhunters
have been around again
and though I've often said
that there's no hurry
a word or two from you
would go down well.

A man gets lonely

talking to strangers
eating grasshoppers
waiting for God.

Love what you've done with the place

I'm trying to write a love-poem about paint.
Well, that isn't strictly true, the poem's about you,
but how could I stand here, sixty-plus, and say
my love is like a red, red rose, or claim that black,
black, black is the colour of my true love's hair;
I would look ridiculous — and you my love are grey.

No, better we stay here, here where our love lives:
dust in our hair from rubbing down rough spots,
flecked with the colours of a score of re-dos.
Time for bed? But I'm trying to write about paint:
how it sticks to the walls, how it covers the things
we brush over; how it makes nothing new

but still freshens the place up a bit.
How we've got several cans in the shed.

Who's there

The play's the thing

It starts with one — one life, one seat, one stage,
one man alone on stage in darkest Elsinore. He has
his face, a way to be, his name, his place in history
assured simply by being there; his ups and downs, his
family tree, he has his own fair share of family squabbles;
a common man, he plays his Hamlet on the streets
against the backdrop of the playwright's preferences:
he knows his place and for a moment there before
the others come he is the sum and total of humanity.

'Enter to him Bernardo'— now they are two. Two men
who, each in his own way, will put the question,
and want to know *who's there*. We answer them
with silence. And so it starts with misdirection,
and men are born, grow old and die, each drawn to life
to be a passing moment, light's movement in the eye,
each with a dream they've whispered in a father's ear;
two Hamlets while the third waits in the wings,
and in the process makes of us an audience.

So we begin. We have our role in this. To cough, to stir,
to make our presence felt, to be the whole completed
spectrum of the universe; to be the one, the now, the I,
the many-headed hydra of his mind: his father's death,
his uncle's smile, his mother's slide from tears to bed
to where the power fills the barrel of her womb, his uncle's
theft of what is his — to be a thing too small, too soon
to stir his consciousness; and so he vacillates and waits
and plays his Hamlet in dark corners of the room.
Until we come most carefully upon the hour, and call him home.

The White Horses

El Caballo Blanco, Wooroloo, WA

Somebody's dream of Spain
died here,
made space among the eucalypts

and left its bones piled high
beside the road
in the summer sun.

Horses once danced here,
proud Spanish horses
white as their bones;
high stepping dancers

playing war games on Sundays
while the ants ate their crumbs
and we ate our cream teas.

The ants picked them clean

the white bones
the white dreams
the white horses.

They have crawled on
the summer sun,
and picked clean the white horses.

16

All Quiet

Erich Maria Remarque knew
that death is death
and that we die
when reaching for a butterfly
as easily as if we charged
the guns.

He knew death finds us
one by one
in no-mans land,
in bed,
or on the street in Nagasaki.

There is no way
to die statistically
in company

when only those alive
can count past one;

or know how high
the bones were piled
at Stalingrad,
how many stones stand
silent at Stoke Poges.

You have to be alive
to find the irony in timing
that gives more weight
to one archduke's demise
than to the death of Wilfred Owen.

Stirlings

Like a short poem
in which each word is perfect, the Stirlings rise
above the prosaic plain:

you can chant their names
(Donnely, Ross and Mondurup)
like a litany

you can climb them
(Barnett and Henton, Gog and Magog)
in your mind

you can wear them down
(Toolbrunup, the Abbey, Mount Hassell)
with your feet

you can read them
(Yungemere, Trio, Success and Bluff Knoll)
like a poem in stone.

Shelf-life

In Drumcliffe churchyard Yeats now lies
(old bones upon the mountain shake)
and greets us all with stone cold eyes
(old bones and a horseman passing by)

He calls out: Poets, learn your trade
(there in the tomb with the dead upright)
Sing whatever is well made
(old bones upon the mountain shake)

On library shelf eight twenty one
(take down this book and slowly read)
twelve books have dwindled, now there's one
(old bones upon the mountain side)

and on that one his name relies
(old bones and a horseman riding by)

These my words...

1.

These my words:
the taste of loaves,

of fishes,
seven there were

and five
that grew,

ate up the
land, consumed
the sea;

and all the wheatfields
on it

and all the fishes
in it.

2.

See how I share
the endless harvest

see how I shift the load
from me to you

watch how I sweep
the residue,

the bits that fell
from other lips,

into these other
baskets.

3.

These my words:
the taste of loaves

and fishes.

A field of wheat
and all the fishes in it.

Afterimages of Family Gatherings

He woke to find
the house locked up,
the evening cleared away,
one small bowl
left on the table;

time drew straight lines
from now to then
and morning opened
like a photo album;

he let the loose leafed days
turn in his hands;
he picked them up
and put them down
at random.

Excess of memory
overflows meaning: we
can drown in charted seas,
lie dead between
the groynes of
friendly harbours —

but now we have time we give
our name to continents.

Breakfast was late, three
generations gathered at one table:
they changed in time
to catch cool southern currents,
he watched the future swim
beyond his view.

Some Statements Concerning What the Wind Does

I.

The wind has torn my feet from my legs,
the wind has torn long strips from the sky,
the wind has torn the dust from the earth,
the wind has torn the shape of a bridge
    from out of the mind of God.

II.

Dust blows through the shape of the bridge.
It touches the sky; the bridge is shredded.
The river decides where I can and cannot go.
    My legs will not take me
    where I cannot go.

III.

Shape comes to term in the womb of the eye.
The river is cool and runs over my feet.
The river is wide and runs over my need.
    Wind, earth, and sky,
    transcend the river.

IV.

The wind moves the earth, and the wind
moves the sky. The bridge is born.
I will cross over to the other side.
    I will find my feet there.

V.

And the wind will teach me how the bridge joins.
And the wind will teach me how the bridge lifts.
And the wind will make me into a bridge
    which is earth and sky
    and lives in the mind of God.

The Map is not the Territory

1. Here Be Dragons

The map is not the territory
the word is not the thing
            Alfred Korzybski

This map that I have used
to line my head
is not the territory, and yet
its folds embrace me
everywhere, its conjured
dragons burn the air,

while margins, edges,
rubbed out bits
where coffee stains
and gods once lived

have slipped between
the eye and brain
to add themselves
to bare terrain.

            *

An analogue reviews
this analogue.
Come sail with me,
we'll cross the Internet

find London Transport
at thetube.com
(a mini sailing to Byzantium).

There, far from nature,
Grecian, stylized,
we take the tube map in
with real-time eyes

and learn the fact,
from half a world away,
that London's trains
are all on time today.

2. Looking for India

Looking for India, Bartholemeu Dias
sailed out of Lisbon, turned left,
sailed south, found the tip of Africa,
and called it the Cape of Storms.
Which suggests the voice of experience

Battered and beaten, he gave up on India,
turned back, sailed north, told them in
Lisbon that the Cape was a problem,
so they called it the Cape of Good Hope.
Which suggests the voice of expedience

Fourteen years later, still hoping for India,
he sailed out of Lisbon, turned left,
sailed south, reached the tip of Africa,
and died in a Storm off the Cape of Good Hope.
Which suggests the voice of irony

Bartholemeu Dias, seeker for India,
wrote in the margin of his page in history:
follow your dreams, try not to let them kill you,
and never forget your first impression.
And that's the voice of reality

3. Magellan

After five hundred years who can pretend
to know his reasons? Motives are moot:
somebody has to be the first to find a way,
go round a world, open a can of worms.

Oh we can talk about commercial advantage,
of changing course to use the winds of change;
or we can speculate on the need to prove
things we already know. But what do we know

about joy, or of sailing away from Spain into
unknown waters? What can we know of such
joy, we who can only speculate on motives,
who have never been first to go anywhere,

who think it's enough to be told that five
ships were reduced to one by mutiny, storm
and starvation, and that he died before
the journey's end? What does that say

of regret, or the earth turning under your bow?
Or that moment when everything changed,
as you felt the waves lift you again,
and a world slipped across your horizon.

4. Antarctica

Stay home, she said. He pushed the cup away
and wind came off the plateau, deeply cold:
black frost on grass, Antarctica at play;
she offered tea, a bun, a buttered roll.

Stay home with me, she said. *A man's estate*
is bounded by the hunger at his door;
stay home and drive the terror from your gate.
Another slice? Please help yourself, do have some more.

No thanks, he shook his head. *It's very nice.*
I'll be a while, he said, *I have some chores.*
And step by step the blizzard took his life.
And one by one the teacups kept the score.

5. Captain Cook

Captain Cook, having outstayed his welcome,
on being brought back piecemeal to the shore,
was boxed as is the custom of his people,
the right words said, and then dropped overboard.

And all his courage wasted on the fishes,
and all his knowledge lost at sea again.
No way to chart the shoreline of his wishes,
sandwiched between the liver and the brain.

6. Armstrong

Nearly a quarter of a million
miles and four days out
from his blue green planet,
he made his landfall
on a dusty plain

fulfilled the collective leap
of the imagination
with a step

and left the words
we come in peace
for all mankind

written in stone
under his nation's flag.

Above his head the blue
green planet turned.
The dust of Cortes
and Pizarro stirred

and somewhere out beyond
the Magellanic clouds,
Atahualpa filled a room with gold
and Montezuma
tore out hearts in vain.

7. Baroque in the Morning

Spring, summer, and autumn each sing,
then winter comes quickly (non molto):

the four seasons flow through my
speakers while the sun rises.

Baroque in the morning: Eine
kleine Nachtmusic to start the day,

Mozart and Vivaldi with the email,
Pachelbel perfect with coffee,

and Bach, perfect Bach, perfect
with everything, everywhere.

He's out there now,
somewhere between the toast

and Alpha Centuri,

and when he makes it back
he'll bring a brand new day.

8. Antipodes

If I sail for long enough
and far enough

and round about enough
and up and down enough

and if I'm tough enough
to think of love enough

and break my heart enough
because I'm not enough

I will reach the Antipodes
somewhere out there

in the Gulf Stream
near Bermuda

(surely enough of an antipodes
for anyone)

and I'll have nowhere

left to go
that isn't home.

Dead Dog in the Road

This much was true: when daylight came the dog
was dead. Its body stiff in early light, coat wet with rain,
its blood and brains still making patterns on the roadside,

its tiny death one among the deaths of passing millions:
the squeal of brakes, the thud, the breaking chain
lost in the pouring down of sound that was the night.

Dog Dead: The Case for War, the headlines read —
and then they dragged us all away, our broken backs,
our shattered chains; our deaths soon lost behind incoming
weather, the roar that always leaves us in the gutter.

This much was true. When daylight came the dog was dead.

In the Borderland

Speaking universally,
taking the view of the moon
you might say,
nothing much happens
in the borderland:

it's just earth,
staid land and static sea,
blue-green simplicity
implicitly believed.

But here in the borderland
slow dunes creep,
sand moves our feet,
waves play with our opinions,

while motile margins
flood and slack,
go out, come back,
make endless indecisions.

Here in the borderland
littoral sands stretch far away,
each grain swept by the waves;

some come, some go,
some try to stay;
some move from past
to pilgrimage.

Maison Galopie

Study: A house, two cars, the weight of light on paper.
The house. Its name. La Maison Galopie.

The house was old. That hard grey stony
kind of old that had no number, just a name
in longhand written on a stone, and though
we'd never know just what its strange name
meant, we came to love its ancient stones;
its twisted inside outside stair, its mossy well
that echoed soft, and far beyond our deepest
reach the plop of pebbles.

Love's touch was soft that year. It brushed
grey walls to mark our presence. White.
White daub with blue mixed in to make
the white seem even whiter; rose-coloured
stone around the door; the keystone locked
in past and future, pink, pale pink, the order
of the day: rose quartz against the unseen blue.
You held the door ajar and drew me in.

The hill. The bay. The names of places.

Sometimes on summer days,
we'd climb the hill behind the house to find
St Pierre-du-Bois spread out in fields below us;
and we would look across Rocquaine to where
the causeway joined L'Eree to Lihou island.
But there was nothing there of ours, a glimpse
perhaps, the view across the wider scene towards
the lighthouse flashing warning of Les Hanois.
But that was everyone's, and in the end was no-one's.

Jaffa. The car. The facts of life.

Burnt orange bright, flat-screened love
of your life, the car in which we met and married,
your car not mine, now grazing, out to grass,
eccentric symbol of a life that waited for me
here, then there — self-branded Val d'Isère,
been there done that you'd say today, but not back then,
back then we simply did it. Bright orange Dyane 6
still part of everything. Except the future.

The house. The past. The moment gone.

Enter a low-beamed hall. Ahead a stair that once
turned out-of-doors, to right the kitchen, set below
the master bedroom, the warmth and winter taken care of:
they brought the livestock in when this was young.
Across the hall, head bumping low, the house
becomes one room, four windows square,
six hundred layered years of papered walls,
of scrapes of paint, of putty knives and hands
that touched the hands of others, that let
the love flow in. It was our turn to lay, re-lay,
to be the cornerstone, to be six hundred years
of dust on hands, to do our bit, to be the loving.

Allegro. Some facts about islands.

Gold dust on glaze, an Inca's dream,
God's sweat left parked behind the orange Dyane.
It sits in space, what can it do, where can it go?
Our car, my car? It is a car that looked the part
until the day we bought it, brought it home
a Sunday drive along the coastal road
which goes around and round-about,
and brings you back here every 40 minutes.
A tiny, very Guernsey, glimpse of hell.
An island is an island, is an island.

The house. An old conclusion.

Upstairs a hall, three rooms with beds,
three windows, bathroom, storeroom, toilet;
a view that slips down to the sea and
down again until the sea goes up, and up
and out, and we can jump to new conclusions:
a different house; a bigger island;
and just enough of history to speak of.

Counting the Swans

I would change nothing.

Not the red beaks
or the black feathers;
not the noise of the freeway,
or the outreach of trees.

But I do not have time ...

Small deaths fill my hours,
give their shape to my days.

And I am counting the swans
in the Lake Monger carpark
counting my hours
in the Lake Monger carpark
red beaks and black feathers
in the Lake Monger carpark
and the dampness of places
I do not have time for;

and I do not have time.

Galapagos

13 ways of looking at a finch

Small ground and medium,
the large ground finch,
sharp beaked in large
and small with cactus on its mind,
lives on the far shored
islands of Galapagos.

Tree finches, medium,
small, upsized, woodpecker,
finch with mangrove eyes,
that warbles, eats no meat
and lies
beyond my understanding,

live here their differences absurd
in such a tiny tiny bird
yet Darwin shaped a brand new world,
its consequences binding.

At Churchill's Funeral

He died in January,
a cold, black and white month in the north.
So we watched as, in shades of grey,
his flag-draped coffin
led the cavalcade
and the empty-saddled horse
along Whitehall,
past one-eyed Nelson
standing on his column,
on down the Strand to Fleet,
the media standing tall,
up to St Paul's.

We'd gathered round 'the box'
to watch these symbols of lost leadership
file through 'the camera'
(I thought the back-turned boots
meant looking back),
while outside, in full colour,
southern summer
yearned for the coming years
and willy-willys
whirred
through open spaces.

'He stemmed the tide with words,'
my father said,
'but would have left us high and dry.'

'Death is a word,'
my mother said,
and closed the blinds
out of respect for death,
the dead,
and summer sunlight
bright as knives
used at a ritual sacrifice.

Scheherazade

When the words stopped

Scheherazade
stopped.

She heard the words,
sinking through layers of silence,

saw them counterweight
the morning sun,

she could not feel
the air vibrating,
she had no sense
of spaces filling.

'I am dead,' she said,
'I am dead and gone.'

*

Scheherazade knows.

She knows the light,
the weight, the threat,
of a morning sun;

knows that words
spoken at breakfast
can eat you for lunch;

she knows a thousand
and one things
that cannot save her

now that the light
has found Schahriah.

'I am dead,' she says,
'I am dead and gone.'

                    *

Scheherazade breathes.

She does not feel
the air vibrating

she has no spaces
that need filling

all that remains
is this quiet
breathing.

'I am dead,' she says,
'I am dead and gone.'

Uncertainty Principle

When we were young to see was to believe,
we knew that sand was white, the water blue;
but then we found that colours could change hue,
which made us think our younger selves naïve.
Now we have learned that time and life deceive:
    that time relates, and life's reality
    is quantum leaps away from certainty
    no matter what we sensibly perceive.
And so once more, finding ourselves at sea,
watching the waves break on a narrow beach,
    we wonder if tomorrow there will be
    anything solid still within our reach —
and if we'll have the strength and will to brave
the leap of faith from wave to breaking wave.

Labels

1.
Ernesto [**Che Guevara**]
in a [**blue black beret**],
and a T-shirt with the message
that [**Bolivia**] is [**to die for**],

navigated [**Nike™**] trainers
through [**Supreme Court**] Gardens

found his way past oleanders
[**by the book**]

and looking like he used to
on the wall
though better dressed
and not so tall

talked a red streak
on a green day.

*Hey [**Che**], I said, you're back*

and I can find no way to say
I'm glad to see ya.

What brings you here today?
*[**Work**] [**pleasure**] [**murder**] [**prey**]*

What's in a
name? they'll say
*[**come the revolution**].*

2.

Ernesto [**Che Guevara**]
in a new [**Oshkosh B'Gosh™**]
[**blue denim**] overall

crossed roads
alone on [**Sunday**]
afternoon

made [**friends**]
with what was left
of [**Sunday mornings**]

chased [**rosellas**] from
the [**Morton Bay**] figs

and on a whim
on a wish

changed [**heart
and mind**]
on a green day.

*Hey [**Doc**], I said, you're dead*

*you don't have even half a shot
at a prognosis.*

*Leave well enough alone
get up, get out, go [**home**]*

*sufficient to the day
its revolution.*

3.

Ernesto [**Che Guevara**]
in a cut down pair
of old blue denim [**Levis™**]

and a T-shirt with the message
that he's been there and
[**tomorrow**] is [**to die for**]

called a meeting
with the [**youngsters**]
on a green and blue
[**true blue**]
gun barrel day;

talked them
the [**Lazarus**] talk

walked them
the [**Lazarus**] walk

breaking all
the pieces
on a green day.

*[**Comrade**] I said*
the waiting lasts forever

and the stars can climb
no higher than the sky.

Get up, go home, play dead
I'll take back all you've said

and everything's going to change…

Winter and Lancaster Gate

In summer parks
the ebb and flow of life
washes against, around, and through
islands of rustic playgrounds;
drowns the dead kings,
the edge of memory statesman,
the forgotten soldiers;
laps at archipelagos of benches,
and pools in picnic sites beside
the war memorials.

In summer parks
the children come and go,
the days and years and decades
come and go,
the joggers, lovers, riders,
come and go,
the music and the picnics
come and go —
there is diversity and sameness
in summer parks.

I have a memory of a winter's day.
There is no ebb, no flow,
only the slow drip, drip of rain on 'Peter Pan',
who plays pretty, pianissimo notes,
lost to the long dead Wendy
(who was a summer child);
and there, across the grass,
where horse and man
are frozen powerfully,
a small boy climbing 'Physical Energy'.

A Rhyme for the Nursery Perhaps ...

Earth bound down
   to bomb blast shelters,
caught in sunlight
   flicker falling,
filling out the open space,
    between
the fight and flight —
dying in their ordered
   thousands,
every name read out.

But who washed away to sea,
    drawn to ancient harmony
rock ground mountains
   tumbled, drowning,
took us in our hundred
   thousands, caught
within the ocean's rhythms,
   currently without.

Who will sing this litany,
   sing this harvest
of the sea, break and bring
   it back to me
dressed in its own geography,
   every name a shout.

Blueprints

In the final days
the pen slipped from his hands
and keyboards froze
beneath the stutter
of his fingertips;

he turned his thoughts away,
and silence filled
the moving cage
of his attention span.

Against the backdrop
of his flickering nights
and days, he watched
the preening of a bird,
a falling leaf

and the ways
that shadows move
became important.

Time slipped his mind,
he touched the edge
of mystery.

Again the bridges grew,
again he made the leap
from here to there.

Job

The way things go these days, who can be sure
of anything? The rivers run then stop, the days dry up,
and I can do no more than wipe the sweat away
and watch the wind take crops that should have fed
the hundred millions and crumble them to dust.

I write in dust, I write the days: a thousand thousand
years in which the wind plays games and yet the slow
earth stays, the rain comes back, and ancient oceans lap
on shores where dinosaurs once ran and children played;
and I remember yesterday as if I'd once had Eden.

What Panther ...

what Panther stalks beneath the earth...
M. Kathryn Black

In the panther's last moment,
when the dull earth erupts
from under the living skin,
when, in the dark of the sky
black roses grow,

raining their petals
on the dark pavement,

we will go to the zoo, you and I,
to the cage of the earth
to the glassed enclosures,
to the drill in the jaguar's eye —
to the place where we save
what is left,

you will find if you walk
past that place,
past that heel on the floor
and the restless
turning — past the crowd
and the look on its face,

past that vision of God
and horizons churning

my face in the glass
of your door, my face
and the glass,
and the roses coming.

Tunnel

Inside the air is fresh, as if great fans still spun.
As if great moths of air, drawn to a distant light
flew through on dim, dark wings, and we, made blind
by that same light can feel their going, can feel
them moving us away towards the day, which we resist,
made darker in this place light never touches.

Walk hand in hand. Trust to the maker's providence.
Trust to the man who made the thing, the pick,
the spade, the iron rail, the permanent way now gone —
although the gradient stays just one-in-eighty here
where the trains once ran, here where we pick our
way with careful steps — there was a hope, a plan,
even a reason given. Is it enough to know that once,
before we came, before we walked this path hope
had its seasons? Walk on — and while the path
is smooth here underfoot it is enough.

The tunnel penetrates. It doesn't tear, it doesn't
steal, it only takes enough to be, yet we can walk
from here into another day, slip like a worm
through earth into the obvious, (already I am two
where once was one) and look — the light has gone.
Walk quickly now, the dark our destination and the sun's.
Outside the air is fresh. As if great fans still spun.

Phoenix

Under the drone of engines I laughed out loud
and flew twelve thousand miles; crossed over
countries, oceans, rivers, seas; looked down on
endless borders. I saw Berlin, Warsaw,
Baghdad and Lahore, their flattened walls, their
new for old confusions; I crossed the Alps, the
Caucasus, the Hindu Kush, and dreamed them all
as waves that fall into a flat brown sea.

I am lost in a white blue white blue white white
sky; I have lost count of just how many lives
have passed me by, how many lives are mine.
The sky is deep in myrrh and ashes.
Cold residues of journeys block my eyes.

Vincent

1. The Road Menders

Do not be deceived by presence.
The tree that dominates the foreground,
the anthropomorphic, unbending
breaker of stones and roads
is not the subject of this painting;

it's just a tree
which, like the other trees
writhing in purgatorial agonies
of autumnal flame becomes
a metaphor for force and time.

Do not be deceived by clarity.
It draws the eye, and shows the broken road
in the subtle angle of a woman's foot;
but she walks to show that need exists,
and is not the subject of this painting.

The subject of this painting is the road menders.

You will find them at the pale centre of things
and among the stones beneath the autumnal trees;
lost in their work, difficult to see
against the background of their lives;
essential in their anonymity.

2. The Red Vineyard

Heat seeps through
autumn's pores, the vineyard
burns; leaves curl,
vermilion flares, the fire dances;

dark purple red
grapes gather in deep
baskets; the earth
achieves, the wine
is poured, the sun is harvested.

The women work knee deep
in burning leaves,
they are complete, forever
here, forever bending;
their bodies hold the angled edge of pain,

which takes their shape, and knows their names,
and counts the days since birth, since dawn,
since time and vine began.

3. Sower with Setting Sun

Hennebicq saw it when it was new
and thought it brutal,
savage, cruel,

the tree menacing,
the sower a massive
brute of a creation—

not art at all.

How everything waits
for the seed to fall.

I see things differently.

I see a broken burnt-out tree
spilling with life,
the supine fields,
a sun grown heavy with light,

a day grown heavy
with the promise of darkness;
and a man
half-haloed by the sun.

He moves through fields
towards the coming night,
a dark, aphotic man
who only sees
the sunlit fragments
of his working day;

he does not see
the sun, the tree, the air,
the symmetry;

or everything waiting
for the seed to fall.

4. Van Gogh's Bedroom

A simple room.

Van Goghs hang on blue walls.
It has blue doors, a brick red floor,
two yellow chairs to welcome visitors.

"Look." says the room. "Can you see
who will sit on the yellow chairs,
who has sat on the yellow chairs?"

"I am here," says a yellow chair,
"I am standing on the brick red floor,
I am waiting for you to understand."

"Look." says the room. "Can you see
who will stand on the brick red floor,
who has stood on the brick red floor?"

"I am here," says the brick red floor,
"Without me the orange bed would fall.
I am waiting for you to understand."

"Look." says the room. "Can you see
who will sleep in the orange bed,
who has slept in the orange bed?"

"I am here," says the orange bed,
"I have a red cover and white pillows.
I am waiting for you to understand."

"Look." says the room. "Can you see yourself here, in me now, at this instant? I am here. I am a room…"

"I am waiting for you to understand."

5. Wheat Field

Three roads, a fourth implied,
a place you cannot see on which to stand,
wheat in the field, crows fly;
the dream must end.

I am this field, these roads,
this darkening sky,
this flock of crows that flies on wasted wings;
I am the need to live, the urge to die;
I dream the dream,
I am the dream that's dreamed.

Three roads, a fourth implied,
a place you cannot see on which to stand,
wheat in the field, crows fly;
the dream must end.

6. Painting 'Dr Gachet'

Still in the moment,
after carefully brushing aside
the hungry eyes, he paints
the things he sees.

He leaves blank the other faces,
the things to be,
the man from Sotheby's,
and the mad sweet air
where Saito burned,
and maybe he'll be there,
or maybe not —

still in the moment,
where all journeys
end,
he takes the brush,
adds Vincent and amen.

Nullarbor

Topography still has its part to play:
burying the sharp edged cheekbones in the earth,
finding old skylines folded into landscape,
following paths to where the thrust gave out
and rock worn smooth and smoother still
hides in an endless oneness the beauty
of lost hills, the soft deceptions
of dry lakes, the ancient valleys' shapes
still shaping earth with rough and casual
skill, gouging with thumbs the skull,
the sockets and the ridge cut through
to where the rivers ran red brown and red,
an endless running downward to the sea.

All that we need is here: the stone,
the hill that is no more, the saltbush plain,
the ever feeding now; the view from
just behind god's eyes — and looking backward.

The Stalling of Birds Observed at Close Quarters

At that exact moment,
seeing the bird
through the reflected
image of himself,

he thought of it,
caught between the cessation
and the beat,

between the earth
and its own soft tethers,
an unexpected phantom in the glass,
hung higher than a cloud has edges.

Rope

a meditation on the death of Atahualpa

If in the end he chose the baptism of rope
what does it matter? God brushed his head
with water dipped in flame, and wrote
the destiny of stars across his forehead.
The rope around his throat became
the outward sign of inward grace,
and as his face contorted till it mirrored
his acceptance of God's will, and then grew still,
the fate of nations turned.

A moment now to look at implications:
five million dead, two million more struck dumb,
the millions still to come, their faces still,
their obligations altered, their pantheons of doubt
and self-deception still at one with God,
whose kingdom come, whose will be done
on earth as it is in heaven, whose will be done
on earth, on earth as it is in heaven.

Ophelia

(A body)
Later we'd look and find her floating there,
hair short, cut like a nun's, the clothes that bore
her up then dragged her down spread all around,
her father dead, her brother so far gone that all he'd
say was 'too much water. Poor Ophelia', or words
to that effect, but first, a reach too far, she came
with songs and flowers to the drowning.

(either wholly)
She came complete, all in one part, so like the willow
tree she trailed her fingers in the weeping water.
A tree too set symbolically to save her,
and yet she sang sweet songs, snatches of tunes —
alas my love you do me wrong but who she sung about,
though we could guess, there was no saying.

(or partially)
She was a mermaid, part scale, part skin,
a fish in air, a woman in deep water,
an owl that once was a baker's daughter
(how what we are becomes all we can be).
She felt a need to drown in water deeper than a puddle,
to trust the sharks, to breathe the deepest seas;
she drowned in air, then drowned again in sorrow.

(immersed)
There's something about being underwater.
Not deep in perspex tubes watching the sharks,
but truly, madly, deeply under water;
the light transfused, you breathe the liquid in

until who knows if you are it or it is you.
Ophelia, mad, can find no reason in it;
can sing no version of it.

(in any liquid)
Drip, drip, the rain's slow song, you are the earth again.
Did we just pull you from the drain to fill a ditch?
Did Gertrude whine sweet to the sweet,
did Yorick really move aside for this?
The shovel pours another blessing on your head.
The jester shares the joke, the limelight, and his bed.

(undergoes an upthrust)
Later we'll put them all away. The shovel in its shed, the tears
that no-one cried, the prayers that no-one took the time to pray,
the things we thought, implied or said, these things we'll pack
inside a play, inside a song we'll give your name. Oh isn't love confusing.
Deep is the ground where love is found; and worms have let the air in.

(or apparent loss of weight)
It seems the air weighs nothing. It seems to slip through lungs
as once it slipped through yours; we breathe you in and breathe
you out again, I feel the willow move in streams of air.
Do your lungs move there in the afterlife? Does your voice
use the earth as once we all used air? The air is still, and we
are all

(exactly equal)
exactly equal

(to the weight)
to the task

(of the displaced)
of being dead.

(liquid)
Goodnight, goodnight, my sweet Ophelia.
Goodnight, goodnight … it's all been said.

Pietà

In response to 'Maralinga', sculpture, Lin Onus, 1990,
The Art Gallery of Western Australia

In this quiet room,
where the dreamtime hangs
in dots of red and black,
in dots of black and white
and fields of ochre,
the light grey walls absorb
the distant thunder
of toxic dreams
we hung upon the wind.

She stands to face the wind,
her clothes cling to her;
her hair, her breath, her life
all blown away; she holds
her daughter close; clings to
a vanished future.

She leaves no space for Michelangelo
or carved Carrara marble; here 'pity'
grows in fibreglass,
and flows
through plexiglass that knows
the shapes we give to progress.

Going Home

Palm trees
lie about climate,
imply twelve month summers
and winter left out in the cold;
stand in rows between
roads and rivers,
road and roads.
Loving dual carriageways, they go to motels
and unload.

Norfolk Island pines,
on the other hand,
never lie about anything except
knowing Abel Tasman,
living near beaches,
and taking tall ships
for a ride.
They lie at anchor on windy days turning
the tides of sunsets.

Furl the sails.
Furl the sails.

The way home follows the road
over rivers
and ends among trees.

Three Reflections from a Broken Mirror

Science Fiction

She stood her ground.
It was as though she was an ending,
a place in time and space
that wanting more
had yet remained quite still,

sufficed, self-mending,
designed by need
to be the shore
on which an ocean breaks.

He turned to go
and in the turning saw a universe,
his thoughts light years away,
the sea not now, not ever
quite enough.

Afterthought

Movement of broom on brick,
the paving stirs, sand trickles
through to points of no return,
makes patterns on
the dark side of the moon.

Why do you turn your face away?
Why do such little things
hold worlds in place?

Alfresco

Naked as sunlight
hands move a teaspoon
the tablecloth stirs:

she is empty
and waiting alone.
She is closed.

When he comes
she will show him
her hands,
each as still as a photograph.

When he goes
she will give him
her bones,
take them off like an overcoat.

Naked as sunlight,
he will think there are reasons
for everything.

Quaraluna, Balkulin, WA, after the reading

1. Three Pictures of a Dam

Last night,
under a moon-white sky
the wind came up out of the east south east;
unexpected,
strong,
it tore the words out of our mouths,
the sparks out of the fires;
it flung quick light
towards the yellow grass.

Yesterday
moon and sun
balanced the sky;
sunset
and moonrise
promised perfection:
we were almost
satisfied.

Galahs flew
over the dam this morning,
moving from north
to south;
grey winged over debris,
liquid pink
on the water,
they crossed the wall,
turned west;

the world in their heads,
the ash and the words
on the ground.

2. Beyond the Fence

Here, on the inside,
where the land
enfolds the water
and the wall
defines its ends,
we are contained
by dimensions of vision,
made tame
by the width of the sky,
reduced by passionate divisions
to a small i.

Beyond the fence
the sky absorbs the eye,
and we are contours
in the flatness of old hills,
old roads that cling
to fading skylines;
caught
in the yellow folds
of the yellow fields
we mutter with the voice
of road-trains,
hold horizons in our hands.

Somewhere out there
the city knows us,
the wheatfields think about us,
the silos fill with grain;

and further south,
where oceans start and end,

Antarctica
begins.

Jerusalem! Jerusalem!

And did that cat in ages past
jump from its box, a spring unwound?
And did it live, or did it not
exactly as true faith propounds?

And did God walk among dead trees
and did he hear them crack and fall,
and did he get the sprung cat back
and leave it there not there at all?

Bring me my Blake, my trusted shield,
my sword of knowledge half acquired;
Bring me the sound of fallen trees,
a cat's cold isotopic fires.

I will not cease from tapping keys
nor would I change creation's plan.
If that box stays I'll leave it sealed:
alive or dead the cat be damned.

Being Born

*"Of the three metamorphoses of the spirit I tell you: how the spirit becomes
a camel; and the camel, a lion; and the lion, finally, a child..."*
*"Who is the great dragon whom the spirit will no longer call lord and god?
'Thou shalt' is the name of the great dragon."*

On the Three Metamorphoses of the Spirit,
from *Thus Spake Zarathustra*, Friedrich Nietzsche.

When I am ready
to be
I will be.

I will look
at the world
with unfocused
eyes

I'll think
about
being born

how it gives shape
to your head

how it can change
your perspective

and when I am ready
to be
I will

I'll be strong.
I'll be strong as the loads
I have picked up
and carried

the roads
I have chosen
and travelled

I'll think
about dirt
and long roads
and the desert
at sunset

about lions and loads
and the burdens of camels

and when I am
ready to ...

I will.

Where will I find you,
bearer of all my ills,
maker of men and lions,
driver of loaded camels,
love in the shape of a dragon
sealed with unspoken rules:

thou shalt not have
thou shalt not keep
thou shalt not want
thou shalt not speak
thou shalt not think
thou shalt not be.

When I am ready
thou shalt not be

when I am ready to be.

And I will look
at the world
through unfocused eyes
and think
about the shape of my head.

Notes

One Tree Bridge

One Tree Bridge is located on the Graphite Road just west of Manjimup, WA. The bridge is actually a single karri tree which was felled across the Donnelly River in 1904; a superstructure was then cut from jarrah trees to form the slabs and decking, making the bridge strong enough to support bullock teams and their wagons. In 1943, the bridge was declared too dangerous for public use. A second bridge was opened in 1948, leaving the old log bridge to fall into disrepair. During a particularly wet and windy winter in 1964, the One Tree Bridge fell into the river and remained there until 1971 when a section of the bridge was pulled out and rebuilt.

Manjimup was named for the Noongar Aboriginal words "Manjin" (a broad-leafed edible reed) and "up" (meeting place, or place of).

Galapagos

The *Geospizinae*, or 'Darwin's finches', are fourteen separate species of Passerine birds. Thirteen reside on the Galápagos Islands archipelago and one on Cocos Island.

"Seeing this gradation and diversity of structure in one small, intimately related group of birds, one might really fancy that from an original paucity of birds in this archipelago, one species had been taken and modified for different ends".

On the Origin of Species, Charles Darwin

Winter and Lancaster Gate

'Peter Pan', sculpture by George James Frampton (1860 – 1928), Kensington Gardens, Hyde Park, within view of Lancaster Gate, London.

'Physical Energy', sculpture by George Frederic Watts (1817-1904), Kensington Gardens.

'Peter Pan' also stands in Queens Gardens, Perth, WA.

'Physical Energy' also stands in Harare, Zimbabwe.

Vincent

I. The Road Menders, 1889.

II. The Red Vineyard, 1888.

III. The Sower (or 'Sower with Setting Sun'), 1888. Jose Hennebicq, Belgian writer, reviewed the painting in 1891.

IV. The Bedroom (or 'Vincent's Bedroom at Arles'), 1888.

V. Wheat Field with Crows, 1890.

VI. Portrait of Doctor Gachet, 1890.

Being Born

The quote is from the translation by Walter Kauffman.

See also theories regarding parallels between Nietzsche's writings and Stanley Kubrick's *2001 – A Space Odyssey* (the symphonic poem *Also Sprach Zarathustra* by Richard Strauss is famously featured in the score of Kubrick's film).

Acknowledgements

Some of the poems in this collection have been published in the following journals and anthologies:

Australian Poetry Journal, vol 2.1, 2012; *Blast,* Issues 4 & 8; *Empowa,* Issues 1 & 2; *Westerly; Touch: The journal of healing* (TLYT Publications, Pennsylvania, US); *Unfamiliar Tides* (2002 Newcastle Poetry Prize Anthology); *Inside Out* (Tombolo Publishing, US, 2004).

Some have also been published online on websites such as *Poetry Downunder, Numbat, Poetic Voices, Oracular Tree, Comrades, Wordspace, Ironwood, Mipo, SCR,* and *Chimera.*

A small number also appeared in the chapbook *One Tree Bridge* (TLYT Publications, Pennsylvania, US), launched in Fremantle, Western Australia, in August 2011.

www.ingramcontent.com/pod-product-compliance
Lightning Source LLC
Chambersburg PA
CBHW030853090426
42737CB00009B/1220